The Six

of a Happy

Marriage

Rev. Medard Laz

LIGUORI
PUBLICATIONS

One Liguori Drive
Liguori, Missouri 63057
(314) 464-2500

Imprimi Potest:
Edmund T. Langton, C.SS.R.
Provincial, St. Louis Province
The Redemptorists

Imprimatur:
+ John N. Wurm
Vicar General of St. Louis

ISBN 0-89243-079-6

Printed in U.S.A.

Table of Contents

Introduction

Not too many years ago, we sang about love and marriage going together like a horse and carriage. For several generations now we have not seen the horse and carriage. And more and more the same fate seems to be happening to love and marriage. Where do we find couples who are growing and who find love in their marriages?

For over two decades tens of thousands of couples around the world have been discovering renewed love in their marriage through the Marriage Encounter, founded in Spain by Father Gabriel Calvo. These Marriage Encounter couples have labored to find more joy in their marriage and so many have found it. These couples are reaching out to help others find a similar love in their daily lives through couple dialogue.

Using many insights gained from the Marriage Encounter experience, this book hopes to challenge couples to go deeper

in their marriage to uncover one of life's priceless treasures —
marital love.

"This one, at last, is bone of my bones and flesh of my
flesh."

Genesis 2:23

1
The Wall

Jamie and Stu — A Typical Marriage

Jamie and Stu always considered their marriage to be good, in fact, better than most. They had their share of crises and arguments, but never what either of them would consider to be a serious problem. Yet their life together was getting noticeably stale. When one of them wanted to go out, the other had more of a reluctant "O.K." They both judged that this was what settling down in marriage led to — on the one hand, faithfulness, commitment, and real sharing; on the other hand, monotony, boredom, and aridness. Theirs was what could be called a typical marriage.

But Jamie would not be satisfied with a typical marriage. She wanted to breathe new life into their relationship. So she decided that next Friday evening she would prepare a surprise candlelight dinner just for the two of them. It would be like the dinners they had when they were first dating — their eyes aglow in the candlelight as they sipped their wine. She could already see the delight in Stu's eyes as she began preparing for Friday night.

On Friday evening everything was ready. Jamie quickly showered, did her hair, and slipped into her new hostess dress. She turned on the soft music, dimmed the lights, and finished preparing the tray of hors d'oeuvres. It was now 6:30 and Stu was due any minute.

7:30 p.m.! She could not believe that the clock in the kitchen said 7:30 p.m. The heat under every pot and pan on the kitchen range had been turned down to its lowest point. As she finally kicked off her shoes, Jamie was at her boiling point. "Where is he?"

8:30 p.m.! All the lights were now out. Then there was the sound of a key turning in the front door lock. "Hey, what's happening?" shouted Stu in his happiest of greetings. "Why is it so dark in here?" he said as he began turning on the lights. "Jamie, what's wrong?"

Immediately Jamie exploded with anger. "I'll tell you what's wrong! Two whole hours I've been sitting here like an absolute idiot waiting for you with supper. Here you are, half lit, not a care in the world. I'm supposed to wait patiently for you . . . not even a call!"

"I really didn't plan on being this late, Jamie. I ran into a couple of guys I hadn't seen in years. They asked me to stop for a beer, so I did. Three times I tried to say good-by, but you know how it is. I couldn't get away."

"So your friends are more important than I am. So are baseball and football, the job, and your rest. I planned this evening especially for us. Five minutes ago I threw all the food in the garbage. It seems that I'm the only one who really cares about our marriage."

"Listen to me, will you, for a change? Listen to me, Jamie. I only had four beers. Here's my uncashed pay check. I'm sorry that I stopped with the guys. I didn't know you had special plans."

"All you had to do was call, Stu."

"Jamie, you're not my mother. I don't have to report to you."

With that, Jamie let out a sobbing scream and ran for the bedroom, slamming the door behind her. Stu tried the doorknob. It was locked. He could hear her sobs, and he felt terrible. He spied the fancy tablecloth and the candles and the gravy soaking through the garbage bag. Angry at himself, at Jamie, and at the world, Stu headed out the door he had entered five minutes ago.

After an hour back at the bar, he called Jamie. The first two times she hung up. The third time she listened to his apology. The tears and the hurt had begun to subside.

"O.K." and "All right," Jamie was finally able to say.

Stu hung up the phone, finished his beer, and headed home. The Friday Night Fight was now over. But a wall had been built . . . a wall that might last for a long, long time.

Both Right . . .

As Stu and Jamie viewed the situation, they were both right. Jamie was accurate in assessing that their marriage needed a boost. Their lives were continually winding down. Her idea for an intimate dinner together was excellent. Everything, except for her husband's presence, went well. She had tried. Stu also was right. He had only stopped for a quick beer. He had tried to leave several times but was pressured into staying. Time just went. He had not planned on being two hours late. Jamie had not told him of her surprise dinner. It had slipped his mind to call. His mother had always bugged him about calling home. He could never stand his mother doing this.

. . . And Both Wrong

Surprise involves risk. When Jamie planned the surprise dinner, she obviously kept it a secret from Stu. Her hopes for the evening were high. With great love she took care of every detail, except one — letting her husband know about being home at 6:30 for supper. His outlook for the evening was ordinary. For Jamie, omitting the element of surprise would lessen the evening. But when communication fails, it is often because something important has not been brought to light. Taking a risk does not always produce the desired result.

Married love means putting the other person first. This may at times seem like slavery, but it really isn't. Stopping for a beer or two with friends can be great. Nonetheless, a courtesy call is often needed — not to check in, or because of jealousy or a lack of trust, but to stay in loving contact with the other person. Where there is no contact, there is no growth. The right words at the right time make many a marriage. Phone calls may cost twice as much today, but they are worth twice as much to many a marriage.

Married Singles

"Married singles" is a term used to describe the sad plight of many people. Two people can become very comfortable in marriage, yet not have a real oneness in their relationship. For "married singles," life is basically the same as before the marriage took place. Both partners come and go respectively to work, recreate, and rest. These are the common grounds and bounds. But the "I's" have it:

"*I* don't have time right now."

"*I'm* exhausted."

"*I'm* always cleaning up around here."

"*I'll* take care of it, don't worry."

"*I* have to get going."

"*I'd* rather not."

Jamie and Stu tossed many "I" statements at each other.
Jamie:

"*I'll* tell you what's wrong. . . ."

"*I've* been sitting here. . ."

"*I'm* supposed to wait. . ."

"*I* planned this evening especially. . ."

"It seems that *I'm* the only one. . ."

Stu:

"*I* really didn't plan. . ."

"*I* tried to leave three times. . . ."

"*I* only had four beers. . . ."

"*I'm* sorry that I stopped with the guys. . . ."

"*I* don't have to report to you. . . ."

I statements are great. But as we will see later, in marriage a husband and wife must go beyond these in order to form a lasting togetherness. A husband and wife must come to discover who the other person is, and where they *as a couple* are in life and in their marriage.

Marriage — Much More Than an Institution

Many young couples enter marriage seeing it as an institution, like the huge church where they were married, or like the spacious hall where they had their reception. To see things in perspective, a couple must consider that the church and the hall took years of planning and building. Just as a fishing license in no way makes one a great fisherman, neither does a marriage license make one a great lover or partner in marriage. Yet we are brought up to expect that, somehow, an engagement and a wedding will do what teachers, marriage courses, and parents leave unfinished in preparing a couple for marriage. Marriage is many things; it is much more than an institution.

Marriage Is a Brick

Though there may be money, gifts, and a big party, all that any couple really gets on their wedding day is a brick . . . a single brick. What is done with it is up to the two of them. They may drop it, toss it aside, or even hit each other with it. Each couple has its own prerogative. The couple is given the brick to be put firmly in place upon the foundation of their courtship and love. Day Number Two of their marriage another brick is given to them with the same prerogatives.

After 25, 40, or 50 years of placing these bricks carefully in the building of the marriage, a living wonder, structured more beautifully than any church, hall, or home, will have been shaped by two loving artisans.

Feelings Tell What Is Happening

Feelings are that deep inner electricity so many people are talking about today. Like electricity, we take feelings for granted. We know that we all have feelings, yet we can't always explain what occurs when the switch is flicked on.

We have millions and millions of feelings about everything, from - chocolate ice cream to Bach, from casual dress to camping outdoors. We may feel accepted or torn, put upon or comfortable, depressed or tingly. The list goes on forever.

Feelings tell a whole lot more than "I'm fine," "That's nice," "O.K.," or "I'm delighted." The feelings you express let me know what's happening with — and inside of — you as a husband and father, a wife and mother. One way or another, feelings eventually see the light of day. The longer they are kept inside, the more difficult it can be for the person to get them out in anything but a negative way. If I am disturbed by your not being on time, and I keep this feeling inside me, I may end up exploding in order to let you know how I feel. Feelings can be buried. In fact, feelings can be buried beneath other feelings. But eventually, even the deepest feelings make their way out — in bedrooms, in the front seat of a car, at airports, at depots, at wakes, or on a golf course.

My Own Feelings

Growing up as a single person, I imitate my parents and my peers. Because of my background with my family and friends, I am impressed with a positive or a negative outlook on life. Upon leaving home, I am still struggling to discover "Who am I?" I have to begin to learn what my real, deep-down feelings are. As a child I may well have felt hurt and unloved as my father drove by the ice cream parlor on a hot summer night, saying that there would be plenty to eat when we got back home. As a teen I often spent money as fast as I could make it on clothes, dates, and a down payment on a car. As an adult I feel pressured to save money, and overwhelmed by the high cost of living.

So much of life growing up was: "Do this — do that" or "Don't do this — don't do that." My feelings, positive and negative, were so tied into my parents, brothers and sisters, teachers and friends, that I really never got beyond the "dos" and "don'ts." But now the important aspect in my life as an adult is not what I *do* (my work, the TV shows I watch, and my sports) but rather — *who I am*. Only when I get in touch with my feelings can I begin to find this out.

My Spouse's Feelings

Each year there are over a million divorces granted in the United States. Add to this the number of couples who separated, and all of those couples living in a dead marriage, and you are talking about an epidemic beyond all proportions!

Epidemics require vaccines. For over a decade now in the United States, Marriage Encounter has offered the vaccine of getting in touch with my own feelings and then sharing them with my spouse.

Mutually sharing feelings for 10 or 15 minutes a day over a cup of coffee, or after the news, or in bed will cause the

daily brick to be put in its proper place. Both partners have to be engaged in the serious business of making the marriage work. This can only be done through knowing and revealing myself — slowly and gradually. A person can scream and shout at a plant, "Grow, grow, grow!" But shouting won't do it. Only air, sunlight, water, fertilizer, and soil help it to grow — slowly and gradually. Plants and all of nature have their natural course for growth. So do people.

A husband may come home from work complaining about the demands of his job and the unrealistic expectations of his boss. Anyone who heard him would get the definite impression that he hated his job. But after dinner and over a cup of tea he shares deeper feelings: that he likes his boss, especially after the compliment his boss gave him that morning; that even though it was a difficult day, he has a sense of having accomplished quite a bit.

A wife may complain about the children fighting and making noise at home all day. Listening to her, anyone would think she had had it with being a mother. But once the children were in bed, she could settle down on the sofa and express how she felt loved as each of her children gave her a bedtime hug and many extra kisses.

Going the extra mile by sharing feelings with one's spouse is so important.

Feelings Are Feelings; Critical Is Critical

Feelings simply *are*. They are neither right nor wrong. Therefore: we should not *judge* feelings — our own, or our spouse's — to be right or wrong.

But we do tend to judge feelings. We tend to do this constantly, without even realizing that we are doing it.

One thing that keeps many people from realizing they are judging feelings is the word *feel*. Many people say "I feel" when they really mean "I judge." In almost all cases, when we say "I feel *that*," we are expressing not a feeling but a judgment we have made. For example:

If a person says "I feel *that* the boss is out to get me," the person is making a judgment, not expressing a feeling.

If the same person says "I feel *put down* and *hassled* almost every time the boss opens his mouth," the person is not making a judgment, but expressing a feeling.

Or take this example:

"I feel *that* these kids need more discipline" — is a judgment. Notice the word *that*. (Sometimes we don't bother to use the word *that*. But if *that* fits into the sentence, there is the clue: we have made a judgment.)

Now take this example:

"I feel *useless* and *helpless* when the kids scream and start hitting each other" — is an expression of feelings. Notice: the word *that* would not fit after the word *feel* in this example.

Criticisms — negative judgments as in the examples above — are often very accurate. But even when criticism is accurate, feelings are not being shared.

In an attempt to improve their situation, some people express judgments to their spouse. For example:

"I feel *that* you should look for a new job."

"I feel *that* you're too easy on the kids."

Both of these statements may be accurate assessments of the situation. But in neither case is there any personal communication of feelings with the person's spouse. To make personal contact, the person has to share feelings, not make judgments. For example:

"I feel relieved and excited when you come home from work."

"I feel warm and excited coming in the door, knowing that the ones I care most about will be there to greet me."

Deep down we all have these same feelings, or similar ones. But they need to be brought to light, and expressed, for a marriage to flourish. The sharing of these feelings is what makes a marriage grow more intimate.

So when your spouse asks you for your outer garment, give your inner garment as well.

A Question of Feelings

This chapter ends with a set of questions under the heading "How Do I Feel. . . ?" *These questions can help your marriage grow.* But they can do this only if you and your spouse sit down and use them to share your feelings with each other.

The best way to use these questions is to *write your answers to them.* Writing helps you to reflect as your words go down on paper. As you write, you focus your mind and concentrate. You give form and expression to the feelings inside you. You find yourself putting down on paper feelings you were not even aware you had. Writing helps you to see inside yourself. It also helps you to share yourself with your loved one. (Chapter 5 has more to say about writing and sharing. If you want, look ahead now to the section "Writing Feelings" on page 44.)

To get as much as you can out of writing and sharing, follow these simple guidelines:

1. *Every day, answer one of the questions below.* It is not necessary to take the questions in the order given. Nor is it necessary to use them exactly as you find them. For example, you might take the fifth question and change it to: "How do I feel when *you* say that *you* are sorry?"

2. *Separately, write your answer to the chosen question.* Put it in the form of a letter; in fact, make it a love letter. Write for a minimum of five minutes, a maximum of ten minutes. Time yourselves with a watch or a clock. Stick to expressing your *feelings,* not judgments or opinions.

3. *Sit together with your spouse and read each other's letter.*

4. *Finally, in your own words, tell each other what you wrote.* Stick to expressing your feelings, not judgments or opinions. The point is to share your feelings — ideally, your feelings about each other here and now.

How Do I Feel. . . ?

First day:	How do I feel about sharing my feelings with you?
Second day:	How do I feel when I offer suggestions to you?
Third day:	How do I feel when I am late?
Fourth day:	How do I feel when you get angry?
Fifth day:	How do I feel when I say I'm sorry?
Sixth day:	How do I feel when I make a mistake?
Seventh day:	How do I feel when you say "No" or "We'll see"?
Eighth day:	How do I feel about the boss?
Ninth day:	How do I feel when the children scream?
Tenth day:	How do I feel about having a drink?

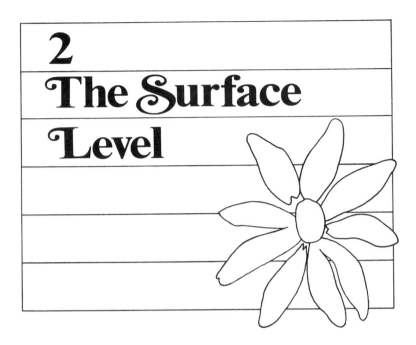

2 The Surface Level

Alan and Betty — The Way Marriage Is

"Come on, Alan, the sale ends today and I'd like your opinion on the drapes."

"Betty, I'm tired, and I just got comfortable."

"But the sale ends today. You had more rest last night than I did. Let's go."

"It's the third quarter and this is a key game. You know what you want. Drapes are your bag, anyway."

"But I'd like your opinion. I've narrowed it down to three choices. We'll be back in an hour."

"My wallet is on the dresser. Just take what you need, Hon. Whatever you get will be fine with me."

Betty senses that the cause is hopeless. She puts on her coat, goes to the bedroom, takes the wallet, and slips out the door. As Betty drives to the store, many thoughts race through her mind: "I guess this is the way things are in marriage. . . . It's not that he doesn't love me, he really does. But I wish he would show it more. He could have come with me if he really wanted to. . . . He was comfortable in front of the TV. . . . The game was too important. Oh, he cares about me, but in his own way. It's just the way marriage is."

Question: Is this the way marriage is, the way it has to be?
Answer: Only if the two people want it to be that way.

Depth in marriage can be described in six stages or levels that all couples are challenged to discover in their relationship. These are the *Surface, Physical, Friendship, Sharing, Trusting,* and *Nonverbal* levels in marriage. If these levels are not initially apparent, the intimacy of life together eventually will call them forth. The following chapters of this book will look at each of these levels to see how much more is possible in most marital relationships.

The Surface Level

When a man and a woman stand before the altar and say, "I will love and honor you all the days of my life," a ship with their names on it is launched upon the sea of life. The greater part of their time and effort will now be directed at providing for their surface or material needs: working, cooking, cleaning, shopping, paying bills, and the like are now "their" responsibility. At the surface of a marriage, providing becomes the primary task of the husband and caring-for becomes the main focus of the wife.

By the time a couple is ready to get married, they have centered their relationship on the surface concerns of their life together — lining up the bridal party, the church, the photographer, the invitations, the flowers, the hall, and the honeymoon. They must get the apartment set up — the painting, the carpet, the drapes, the furniture, and the utensils. Surely all of this needs to be done, but it centers a couple at the surface level of their relationship. Lists are compiled and are forever being checked off to see what progress is being made, what tasks are being completed.

Soon a marriage and a relationship can become identified with these lists of things to be done. This generally gives a false sense of accomplishment. For, once married, the lists continue in an even greater number: washing windows, doing the income tax, shaking out the rugs, shopping, fixing the car, ironing, cleaning, etc.

Questions Couples Ask

I was in the audience years ago when the late Elvis Presley made his comeback in Las Vegas. I wound up sitting at a table with four couples that I soon discovered were newly married. I was greatly enjoying the evening and the entertainment on stage. But in the course of the entire evening I heard many comments whispered into a spouse's ear. . . .

"Did you see to it that both of our names got put on the checkbook?"

"Did you tell Mother and Dad what hotel we were staying at in case something happens?"

"Did the waiter say anything about how much the drinks are costing?"

"Do you have the credit cards with you, or are they up in the room?"

These comments are not unique to the honeymoon. For many couples, these kinds of remarks represent the sum and substance of their marriage relationship. These are the things that they heard in their growing-up years. It is assumed that these are the important matters in the marriage that will keep it alive and going.

Where the World Is

The world exists at the surface level of life — what can be enjoyed, eaten, smoked, worn, driven, visited, seen, and heard. These have become the really important aspects of daily living. And these values are passed along to those who get married. . .

"How's the new car?"

"Did you see Marsha's new hairdo?"

"Going anywhere over the holidays?"

"We just bought a new house."

"I just love that new restaurant."

At and apart from work, communication runs along these lines. Success and personal worth are judged by such statements and how individuals respond to them. Success in marriage is often judged in similar terms. . .

"What kind of a vacation can we afford?"

"How much did we save last year?"

"We can't afford to have a baby."

"I really want that promotion."

"It's our turn to have the neighborhood party."

It is so easy to think that life is passing you by when a neighbor says over the backyard fence that she has just returned from Jamaica when you have just gotten back from McDonald's.

The world changes. Neighborhoods are torn apart, cars become junk, and money has a way of being spent. If marriage turns on the same axis as the world, disaster is imminent. Marriage must go deeper than the surface or the material.

Marriage is judged a success when we have more, when we've provided. Yet using this surface level as a measuring stick is dangerous, because everything is then measured in dollars and cents. The surface level does not provide any deep inner peace. There is always tomorrow's work, another meal to cook, traffic to fight, diapers to change — a never-ending go-around. Success and a sense of accomplishment are very fleeting. Children, because of many material demands, can keep a couple at a surface level in their relationship. A couple will change residence to secure a backyard and to provide a better neighborhood and education.

A Revolving Door

Marriage at the surface level can become like a revolving door. The husband and wife keep going round and round. They can see each other. But they must keep on moving. In truth, they are really going nowhere. There is no close contact, even though they are side by side. They cannot adequately hear each other. They cannot even touch each other. The surface level of a marriage has the distinct knack of putting two people in a revolving door that goes round and round. This may well be Alan and Betty's situation in the example cited above.

The Next Step — Real Contact

A husband and wife must become more than mere characters on the stage. For example, after they have spent all day painting walls together, it is easy to assume that they have been in contact with each other. But very often that is not the case. To get into real contact, the two painters ought to sit down, even before the paint brushes are cleaned, and share. For example:

"I felt a freshness, a new life in the room, as the paint was going on. I feel happier already."

"I watched my dad paint many times. He never trusted me to help much. He didn't want me to upset him or the can of paint. I've never liked the smell of paint. But today it was O.K. It was even fun. I felt a new closeness to you. I'm proud of the way we've made the room turn out."

In moments like this, real contact happens. The masks come off, fears subside, hostilities are forgotten, anxieties over the project are released, and true enjoyment can now happen.

Two people in the same room all day can be involved in the same project, yet both can be feeling very differently about it. They can deepen their marriage by sharing these

feelings. But often this next step is not taken. Instead, they move on to another surface activity, such as:
"I've got to get cleaned up."
"Let's eat."
"Let's move the furniture back."
In other words, "Let's reset the stage." But then, when will married life happen? Only when the next step of sharing feelings happens.

Roles and Feelings

It is at the surface level that roles are played out. Society has been changing in recent years. As a result, the husband's role is not merely that of breadwinner and the wife's that of homemaker. Nowadays, the wife may have a job that provides as much or more income than the husband's job. The husband may baby-sit the children frequently and do many other household tasks. But this is merely a switching and an overlapping of roles. The roles are still played.

The important consideration is *not* who is "The Provider," "The Strong One," "The Cleaner Upper," "The Organizer," or "The Accountant." The important question is: "How do you feel in playing each of these roles in the marriage?" When spouses tell how they feel, their answers are revealing. For example:

"I hate always having to be 'The Strong One.' Sometimes I'd just like to scream — just to get some notice for myself. Then I tell myself that I have to be strong."

"At times I'm overwhelmed by the financial responsibilities of providing. At lunch they were talking about the cost of college. It frightens me. After lunch I had to bite my lip rather than speak my mind to the boss. I want to protect the job I have."

Roles can be played only up to a point for actors and actresses, and also for husbands and wives. When I tell my spouse how I really feel, I outgrow whatever role I have and become a true lover.

A friend of mine sneezed at work one day. He folded up his handkerchief and was about to replace it in his pocket, when he noticed how cleaned and pressed it still was. In almost 30 years of marriage he had never noticed the handkerchiefs he always carried. For years his wife had been spending time and effort ironing his handkerchiefs. And for years he had overlooked this sign of her love that was, literally, right under his nose. The first thing he did when he came home from work that evening was to give his wife a big kiss. Then he thanked her for the love she had put into doing his handkerchiefs all those years.

How Do I Feel. . .?

Note: Every day, answer one of the questions below. (Change the question to anything you want.) Separately, write your answer to the chosen question. Sit together with your spouse and read each other's letter. Finally, in your own words, tell each other what you wrote.

First day: How do I feel about going shopping with you?

Second day: How do I feel about watching TV?

Third day: How do I feel when I think about my responsibilities as a married person?

Fourth day: How do I feel when I have to do housework?

Fifth day: How do I feel about saving money?

Sixth day: How do I feel about success in life?

Seventh day: How do I feel when the children make demands?

Eighth day: How did I feel the last time we finished a household project — like painting the house?

Ninth day: How do I feel about the roles I play in our marriage?

Tenth day: How do I feel about the little things you do for me?

3
The Sexual
Level

Milt and Olive — Closer Together

Quite frequently Milt and Olive went to visit Milt's parents on Sunday afternoon. After dinner Milt would sit with his dad and brothers and watch the game on TV. Faithful to their ritual, the men spent the afternoon in front of the set, cheering their respective teams. Meanwhile, Olive, Milt's mother, and his sisters would prepare and clean up after the meal, or sit in the kitchen chatting over coffee.

Riding home in the car one Sunday evening, Milt asked Olive how she liked their day. "It was O.K.," she said in a pleasant tone of voice, saying nothing more. The music on the radio played on. Olive's thoughts drifted ahead to Monday morning and getting the children off to school. Milt's thoughts went back to their day and how his "little" sister was now getting ready to begin high school.

"Gee, your sister is getting big," said Olive. "It's hard to believe she was born when we were still dating. How do you feel about not having a little sister around your folks' home any more?"

Milt shared Olive's amazement over his sister growing up. As Olive went on to talk about what the women in the kitchen said that afternoon, Milt found that he was really interested.

By the time they arrived home, their two little ones were asleep in the back seat and Olive was sitting six inches closer to Milt. When she put her arm around him in bed later that night, he responded with a youthful passion.

This story shows how separate a couple can be, even though they are together on a day of rest — he in the living room and she in the kitchen. The front seat of the car might as well have had a partition down the middle if the conversation had gone no farther than "It was O.K."

By touching upon something dear to Milt's heart, Olive opened the door and Milt was able to move in. In bed they were able to culminate sexually the togetherness they had in the front seat of their car. As a popular banner proclaims: "You have touched me and I have grown."

No Problem — Or Was There?

I have filled out hundreds of questionnaires with people seeking to have their marriages annulled by the Church. One of the questions asks: "Did you or your first spouse experience any physical inability to have normal sexual relations during the marriage?" I cannot recall a single person responding "No" as I initially asked the question.

A later question on the annulment form asks: "What is the reason why you suspect that the marriage being contested was never binding, or can be dissolved?" The vast majority of people respond to this question: "There was no deep communication between us. It was all so mechanical." When

I inquire if this was also true in bed, the response I most often receive is: "Oh, definitely! It was just a physical release, there was no tenderness at all."

Sex Is Neutral

Sex is not only natural, it is also neutral. All higher forms of animal life engage in sex. Sex gives pleasure, and keeps a species going. But the meaning of sex is whatever meaning the two people give to it. It can be nothing more than a physical act. Or, it can be a loving response: "Love me as I am, make me feel wanted and loved. Hold me, heal me." Sex can be used to heal or to turn a life in a whole new direction. But sex is not a substitute or an artificial sweetener, like saccharin. Some of the world's greatest strangers are found in bed.

Sex Is Communication

Sex is me, not a part of me, not something added on. Outside of marriage I can give my time, my opinions, my efforts. In marriage I must give myself.

When I say that I love you, I must define my love for you, for today, for now. Greeting cards pour off the presses. We buy them and use a stranger's words to declare love. But love in marriage is not generic. It cannot be put on a counter in a store alongside "Graduation" and "Sympathy."

"I've just had four hours of the kids' screaming."

"I've just wrestled with the biggest business decision of my life."

Although frayed, my emotions have to be slowly unraveled:

"I love you . . . for your struggling . . . for putting up with the kids. I love you with your somberness . . . with your quietness . . . for your sweetness . . . for your torn-apartness."

"In you I see me. When I give you myself, I want a self in return. It's only fair. Please be tender. Tell me what I mean to you today, right now. After the day we've had — torn apart and apart — help heal me. Somewhere along the way today, I lost a self. Help me to find me."

Sex Is Honesty

Sex can easily become routine when it is not honest. When sex becomes merely the release of passion, energies, or tensions, it has lost its dimension of honesty.

Studies and reports have pointed out that the most unfulfilling part of marriage for many couples is sex. This is the direct result of poor communication, of not sharing their deeper feelings about a myriad of daily experiences. It is rare that a couple will sit down and honestly discuss their feelings about their sex life — their inhibitions, background, or temperament. This is because most people feel uncomfortable discussing sex. Often there is a poor background from family and schooling in matters sexual. Early in marriage there is often uncertainty about what to expect sexually. "What kind of a sexual lover do I see myself as?" "How do I see you as a sexual partner?" All too often there are feelings of sexual inadequacy. This can lead to a basic dishonesty in sex. For example:

"Not now, the children are around. They will hear us."

"I'm tired."

"I've got another load of laundry to do."

"The late movie sounds like it should be good."

The old adage, "Honesty is the best policy," here too prevails as long as it is an honest sharing of feelings.

I enjoy when. . .

. . . you cling to me so tightly that I can hear your heartbeat.

. . . you massage my back with your tender touch.

. . . you play with my hair and roll your fingers around in it.

. . . you gently touch my cheeks and give me one of your special wet kisses.

. . . we share one cigarette and we talk after we've made love.

Sex Is Intimacy

Intimacy is a slow, delicate unraveling of self, a stripping of self for the one I love. Intimacy is not a matter of a few seconds or minutes of love-making. Intimacy, like marriage, takes a lifetime of revealing. Each day there is a new chapter in the love story. I become transformed by love. I am so different from what I started out to be in life and marriage that I don't recognize myself. There is such a down-deep peace. My fondest dreams are coming true in a daily way. I am not the same person any more. I can't believe that I've become the lover I am.

Sex Is Love

Sex is love. This is not what the world says when it proclaims: Love is sex. For the world is in the business of selling sex, of trying to sell love. But the world has it all wrong: Sex is love.

When the world says that love is sex, it gives but one meaning to it. Sex and love become all too narrow. The human person, so brilliant and creative, is being limited to a single definition of love. Is that all there is to love? Is there but one way for me to express myself as lover with another person?

I believe that there is an infinite number of ways for a couple to experience and express love. Some are highly sexual, others are less sexual. All of them are love. "There is no limit to love's forbearance, to its trust, its hope, its power to endure. Love never fails" (1 Cor 13:7).

Infinite is too intangible a word. So here are not an infinite number of ways, but a hundred ways I have found for expressing love:

Flash you a smile.
Squeeze your hand.
Listen to your gripes.
Rub your back.
Fix you a cup of coffee.
Buy you flowers.
Ask you how you are feeling.
Show interest in your job.
Offer you a piece of candy.
Tell you that you have pretty eyes.
Fix you supper.
Take you for a drive.
Send you a surprise greeting card.
Write a poem about you.
Invite you to watch TV.
Ask you to dance.
Take you to a movie.
Let you use my tennis racket.
Watch the children while you do shopping.
Fix your flat tire.
Visit you in the hospital.
Hold you as you cry yourself to sleep.
Open the car door for you.
Hold onto you in the labor room.

Call you to cheer you up.
Tell you how important you are to me.
Remember our anniversary.
Share my popcorn with you.
Give you a lift to work.
Take a walk with you.
Wipe away your tears.
Try to understand how much you hurt.
Share with you the latest book I've read.
Take you to a new restaurant.
Send you a Valentine card.
Tell you that everything will be all right.
Help you carry in the groceries.
Shake out the rugs.
Go to see your mother in the hospital.
Share my inner feelings with you.
Call you up just to say "Hi!"
Remember you in my prayers.
Go and help a friend of yours.
Give you the benefit of the doubt.
Tell you that I really believe in you.
Pick up a gallon of milk for you.
Not try to change you to what I'd want.
Clean the kitchen for you.
Take your picture.
Get you a new scarf.
Try to be loving when you want to talk until 1:00 a.m.
Patiently listen to your heartaches.
Take you to the airport.
Dry the dishes.
Take you out for New Year's Eve.
Invite you to go bike riding.
Share a new recipe with you.
Send you a post card when I'm out of town.
Say nice things about you to others.
Be proud of being with you.

Care about all that makes you happy.
Have the house looking neat for you.
Ask you about the children.
Take you shopping.
Bring you a pillow.
Cheer you up.
Miss you when you are away.
Introduce you to people at work.
Let you know that I have time for you.
Fix you a drink.
Clean out the car.
See to it that you are satisfied.
Give you my more "pleasant" self.
Tell you your hair looks great.
Help you balance the checkbook.
Stop with you for ice cream.
Ask you what you're worried about.
Try to hold my temper.
Tell you more about my job.
Stop to look at the sunset with you.
Go without dinner to lend you a hand.
Try to understand what about you bothers me.
Let you know what I'm really afraid of.
Clean off the ice from your windshield.
Give you the more comfortable chair.
Ask you how you liked the evening.
Put my arm around you.
Carry out the promise I made to you.
Call the insurance company for you.
Get up at night when the baby cries.
Give you a warm kiss.
Check to see that you are well.
Empathize with you over your cold.
Try to build up your confidence.
Be on time for you.

Write you a love note.
Leave the soap dish dry in the bathroom.
Wait patiently when you are late.
Put away the laundry.
Tell you that I love you.

How Do I Feel. . . ?

Note: Every day, answer one of the questions below. (Change the question to anything you want.) Separately, write your answer to the chosen question. Sit together with your spouse and read each other's letter. Finally, in your own words, tell each other what you wrote.

First day: How do I feel when we go to visit our families?
Second day: How do I feel about riding in the car with you?
Third day: How do I feel when there is silence in the car?
Fourth day: How do I feel when you tell me that you love me?
Fifth day: How do I feel when you get upset?
Sixth day: How do I feel about discussing our sexual life?
Seventh day: How do I feel about our sexual life?
Eighth day: How do I feel when you are close to me?
Ninth day: How do I feel when you respond to my sexual advances?
Tenth day: How do I feel when I make sexual advances to you?

4

The Friendship Level

Bretta and Derek — The Early Bird and the Worm

A typical Saturday morning dawns as Derek is up early, putting a pot of coffee on the stove. He has always been a morning person. He pours a cup of coffee as he sits down to figure out his projects for the day. He then heads off to be one of the first shoppers at the local hardware store. This is his normal ritual for a Saturday morning.

After the rigors of her week, Bretta enjoys sleeping late on Saturday morning. She is by no means a morning person. Saturday often begins for Bretta around noon.

As Derek approaches his car with the things he bought for his outdoor work, he spies a rather pronounced dent on the side of the car. Whoever backed into his car failed to leave a note, which makes him only more angry. With his mind on the cost and inconvenience of putting the car in the repair shop, he drives for several blocks before noticing the flashing police car lights in his rear-view mirror. After getting a ticket for speeding, Derek shops in angry silence. Arriving home furious, Derek grabs one of the bags from the back seat. The bag rips and there is a crash as a bottle of weed killer breaks at his feet on the driveway. Derek storms into the house, now livid over the fact that his wife is just getting out of bed. Where was she when all of this was happening? Sleeping! Every Saturday he is up and going, and she is in dreamland!

"Hi, Hon," says Bretta as she sits on the bed rubbing the sleep from her eyes.

"Why don't you just sleep all day! I'm going to the ball game!" Derek shouts, slamming the door behind him.

Bretta sits there aghast.

As things started to go wrong for Derek that morning, his anger began to focus on his wife. Why wasn't she up, doing things, suffering along with him? Why did she sleep until noon on Saturday instead of having breakfast ready for him?

The basic truth is that Derek and Bretta are different, sometimes very different. Derek is a morning person, up and doing things. Bretta is an evening person, who likes to stay up late. In the morning, if she can, she enjoys sleeping late. Throughout their marriage there will probably be little change in these habits.

Growth as Friends

In marriage, a couple grows in friendship by enjoying the other person just as he or she is. Friendship cannot take place if we try to change each other. As a friend, Derek has to recognize that he is different from his wife, that she is different from him. He has to discover that his day with his wife can begin again at noon. Then, as friends, they can sit down and have coffee together, and begin Saturday as a couple.

Then, over coffee, Bretta can see her husband as a friend — and care about what he has been up to that morning. Some

Saturday mornings she may even roll out of bed and have breakfast ready for him when he returns from shopping. But when she does this, it is not because she has to, or because Derek has been complaining, but because she loves him.

No Compromise

Most couples getting married believe that a good marriage is mostly a matter of compromise: "You can go bowling if I can go shopping. You do the inside cleaning, I'll do the outside work. You can go golfing today, but tomorrow I want to go to visit my folks." Some matters can be worked out amicably this way, but many cannot. Besides, these trade-off arrangements do not deepen friendship. The following are examples of how not to deepen a marriage:

"I'll sleep late this Saturday, you can sleep late next Saturday."

"You can discipline the kids this morning, I'll do it this afternoon."

"I'll watch the first half of the soap opera, you watch the second half of the ball game."

"I'll fix lamb for supper tonight, spaghetti and meatballs tomorrow night."

For someone who sleeps late, is easygoing with the children, loves soap operas, and cannot stomach lamb, compromise is no answer. What is?

Understanding Is the Key

All too often we merely tolerate our spouse's behavior: "Why is he up so early making noise?" "How can she waste half a day staying in bed?" We tolerate another when we use phrases like:

"We'll see."

"Later."

"How many times do I have to tell you. . . ?"

"Let's go."

Withdrawal or avoidance is another way of tolerating one's spouse. Sleeping, drinking, socializing, working, taking a walk can all be means of avoidance.

But, like compromise, avoidance is no answer. What is? The key is understanding. I can come to understand why the other person is the way he or she is through serious dialogue and the sharing of feelings. And once I understand the other person, I can begin to accept the person as he or she is, not as I want him or her to be.

For example, it makes a difference when Derek listens to the following:

"I feel like I'm in heaven when I sleep late . . . to have the world around me get up and get going and, once a week, not to have to rush with it. I remember once when I was a small child, my sister pushed me out of bed because she wanted to play. Mom yelled at her to stop. She said that I needed my rest, that it was good for me. Ever since then, sleeping late on Saturday is a luxury I take advantage of."

And it makes a difference when Bretta listens to Derek:

"I like early mornings and a fresh start. I can't wait to get going, even if I'm tired. I hate to waste those precious early hours before the kids are up, making demands. I like to get things accomplished, and I can, early in the morning."

Understanding the feelings of the other is the key to friendship in marriage. Both husband and wife will no doubt continue on with their individual life styles. But now there is understanding:

"We're different, but that doesn't mean that we are enemies."

"That's why we are friends — we are different, but we understand each other and *why* we are different."

No walls exist between friends. Understanding makes sure of this.

If we were given a fine musical instrument and told that we soon had to perform in a concert hall before a huge audience, we would practice every day. For anything to succeed, work is needed. Marriage is no different. Somehow marriage tries to avoid the work that is needed. Many marriages stop with the surface and the sexual levels and go no further. A marriage really begins to be fun at the friendship level. Here is where two people truly meet and fall in love many, many times over.

Dialogue: A Thing of the Heart

Dialogue is the sharing not only of minds but of hearts. Dialogue is the feeding time for lovers. A friend told me that the longest journey he has made in his life was 13 inches — the distance from his head to his heart. Expressing what is in our hearts is the goal of dialogue. This is not easy. For many this may well be the longest journey of a lifetime.

The only guarantee of success for marriage is faithful, daily dialogue. This is not a time to solve problems or discuss family needs. This is a time for *us,* like when we were first going together and became engaged. Couples who have made a Marriage Encounter have found that they need 10 to 15 minutes of daily dialogue to keep their marriage alive and growing.

A marriage can wear on and on with few changes, and become dull and routine with little excitement. Children growing up in this kind of atmosphere are sometimes asked before they themselves get married:

"Would you get married if you knew your home life was going to be like your parents'?"

Most try to avoid the question by not responding affirmatively or negatively. Instead, most say:

"Ours could never be like theirs . . . because we LOVE one another." It is the defining of their love that two friends in marriage must attend to. Adam and Eve surely had their communication problems, and so do we today. Defining that love takes daily dialogue.

Staying in Touch

Friends maintain their friendship and see it grow by staying in touch. In marriage, staying in touch may be a note in the lunch box saying, "Hope you enjoy this. I'm thinking of you. I can't wait until tonight." A call to or from work — not to report a child's accident, but to say "Hi, how's your day going?" — is a declaration of loving friendship.

Making time for dialogue is essential. Couples with irregular hours and spouses that travel still make time for dialogue, even if it is midnight. Dialogue is what keeps them and their marriage going. If there is a set time — after supper or after the news — then it is looked forward to and can be enjoyed. Each couple has to determine the time that is best for them.

Support in Married Friendship

Support in marital friendship differs from support in other types of friendship. In nonmarital relationships, support goes from the unknown to the known. People become friends because they work together, ride in the same car pool, bowl, golf, or recreate together. These friendships may deepen over time, and then more personal matters may be discussed. Through common interests, two people get to know each other while dating, find enough in common, and marry.

Marriage changes the relationship. In marriage, support goes from the known to the unknown. After months or years of marriage, a spouse says, "I know everything about him, from his wants to his weaknesses." Having possessed the other sexually, we "know" the other person in the Biblical sense.

The challenge of marital support in friendship is that of perspective. "Now that I know this person, I am beginning to see what he (or she) sees in our life together, I am starting to share his (her) vision. It *is* good at times to just sit back and relax . . . camping can be fun . . . saving money really is a problem . . . I can really enjoy gardening." A continuing interchange of perspectives does produce a common vision for friendship in marriage.

Accepting, caring, and loving me just as I am should and must happen in a marital friendship — even if I am 20 pounds overweight, balding, quick of temper, or a slow starter.

So often this support is given by not merely hearing what the other person is saying but by really listening to the person. As a relationship grows, the tendency is to turn the other person off or to expect the expected. Behind all of the words and emotions, what is the person trying to say? When I respond at the same level, not with a mere "O.K." or "Sure, sure," then I am really being supportive. Once we get to know someone, we tend to feel that is enough. We tend not to really listen to the person any longer. "When you listen to me, you take me as I am — faults, ramblings, and all." Of such is friendship. Of such is love.

How Do I Feel. . . ?

Note: Every day, answer one of the questions below. (Change the question to anything you want.) Separately, write your answer to the chosen question. Sit together with your spouse and read each other's letter. Finally, in your own words, tell each other what you wrote.

First day: How do I feel when you (or I) sleep late?
Second day: How do I feel when things go wrong at home?
Third day: How do I feel when we have a cup of coffee together?
Fourth day: How do I feel about accepting you just as you are?
Fifth day: How do I feel about understanding your feelings?
Sixth day: How do I feel about having this daily dialogue with you?

Seventh day: How do I feel about a daily call just to say hello?

Eighth day: How do I feel about listening to what you are saying?

Ninth day: How do I feel when you (or I) say, "Let's go"?

Tenth day: How do I feel when you don't say anything?

5
The Sharing
Level

Earl and Fran — Home and Away

Earl is a carpenter. Throughout the good working months he is out on the job and hard at work soon after dawn. Putting in a full day outdoors, he arrives home physically exhausted. He likes spending time with his wife, Fran, and their five children. During the week, and usually on weekends, he likes to go to bed early.

With five children, Fran is tied to the house, except for trips to the supermarket or to school. She enjoys going out evenings, mostly to classes and discussions where she can learn to understand and enjoy life more. Earl sees her need to get out since she is cooped up all day at home. He is glad to watch the children and enjoys the time alone with them.

But Fran does not like going alone. She wants Earl with her and begs him to go. Often he tags along, but is noticeably bored by these gatherings. Midway through the evening his head starts to bob and Fran often gives him a not-too-gentle poke. On occasion Earl is known to draw attention to himself by a loud snore in the middle of a lecture.

Having made a Marriage Encounter, Earl and Fran were able to write down and share how they felt about going out to meetings in the evening. For the first time in over 20 years of marriage a deeper sharing took place. Earl wrote to Fran:

"I really feel uncomfortable with the people there. I've tried for years to get at their level, but my approach to life is as a carpenter and we don't have that much in common. I enjoy the evening out with you and I'm delighted when a new idea flashes in your eyes. I hope I don't sound like I'm making excuses, but I truly am tired after work. I enjoy the precious time I have with the kids when I can relax and get to know each of them better."

In her letter to Earl, Fran wrote:

"Going out for me to share ideas and to learn is so important. I find that I can dry up just being at home with five children. After a while I begin talking and acting like them. I need to see life as an adult. I need the companionship of my husband. We will be together long after the children are gone."

Once Earl and Fran more fully understood each other, there was much less resentment when Fran wanted to go out. Earl now felt better saying "No," and she felt better knowing he would enjoy himself with the children while she was gone. On occasion Earl was more awake and would go with her and would get something out of the evening — because he wanted to be there. He developed the habit of setting the alarm clock since he often fell asleep on the sofa. He would have his nap then get up and make coffee. When Fran arrived home full of ideas and enthusiasm, he would enjoy hearing about all she had experienced.

Writing Feelings

It is important to express feelings in writing before sharing them. Writing gives time for reflection as the words go down on paper. Most couples form a deep relationship in their engagement by writing love notes to each other regularly, whether they live two blocks away or across the country. The written word between two lovers is personal and reflective. How sad it is that the writing so quickly stops once they are married. A beautiful form of sharing is neglected. In counseling couples whose communication has all but stopped, I have asked whether they wrote to each other while they dated. The usual reply was: "Oh, yes, several times a week." I have sent couples home to get out those letters and read them. Reading their own letters from their dating days, couples experience once again that dialogue in love is possible. But to recapture that artless art, they must begin again to write and to share. Dialogue is most beautiful when it takes the form of a love letter.

Many couples write one word on their calendar that they will use as a topic for dialogue: "Work," "Rest," "Sex," "Shopping," or "Cleaning." A word or a phrase becomes the topic they write on and then share.

As was suggested in Chapter 1, dialogue does not make judgments. But avoiding judgments is not easy. The best way to avoid them is to leave unsaid any sentence in which the word *that* would follow "I feel." Write "I feel," then follow it with a feeling word. (See the list of feeling words at the end of this chapter.)

Rediscovering the Past

A couple has the unique opportunity to rediscover their past by deep sharing. Their memories are weighted with past events, all laden with feeling. For example, the birth of a child can be a harrowing time for both wife and husband.

When the baby finally comes, the joy and relief are almost too much to take. Much is felt — little is said. Even years later it is so beautiful to write and share:

"How I was pulling for you and the baby in labor. I'd squeeze your hand, but I felt so helpless. All the pain you were going through. I kept thinking about how easy men have it, not having to get pregnant and deliver children."

"I felt so close to you in the labor room. I wanted to give you the greatest gift of my love — a child. I was beyond the pain and the hurt. That would soon be over. I was almost giggling with the joy of our enjoying our little one. And he is such a beautiful gift to us both."

Moving into a new house can also be hectic and time-consuming. Two people can be like strangers to each other while engulfed in such an undertaking. This is not to say they do not have feelings about it:

"I was so scared in the house without the furniture, the drapes, and the rugs in. I didn't know a soul, not only in the neighborhood but in the whole city. And you were traveling or commuting all the time. I cried myself to sleep so many nights. I wanted the house, but I never imagined it would be like that."

"I felt like a vagabond. With the traveling and the commuting, every day I laid my head on a different pillow or fell asleep on the commuter train. Wow, was I embarrassed and angry at myself when I fell asleep on the train and missed my stop. The conductor woke me up at the end of the line. You were there, as always, at the stop wondering where I was. Did I feel silly having to call you."

Bringing back feelings from the past is like finding a treasure that has existed for years right under your nose. Life's experiences are so pressured and rapid that they get buried. What a pity! Therein lies the struggle, the richness, and the quality of life together. How can we begin to learn who we are today, how can we chart our tomorrow, without the past? Wondrous feelings are locked in the past waiting to be found with the stroke of a pen or pencil.

Sharing Failures

Sharing failures or a sense of failure is also important. Much of married life embodies dreams. Dreams are easy to come by, hard to get by. "Young men may dream dreams, old men may see visions," but how about the rest of us?

"I feel uncomfortable in a furniture store. I see all the things you like and I want to get them for you. I feel inadequate with the amount of money I make. 'Let's go, let's go' is so often my way of saying, 'I feel like a failure.' "

"Shopping for new furniture is often my way out. I see the new things the neighbors have. Then I get jealous and want new things too. I set my mind against reupholstering, though I know it's the practical thing with our children at the age they are, always spilling milk and soda pop. I worry about the kind of homemaker I am if the furniture isn't decent."

No one likes to admit to failure. And none of us are really big failures. Yet we set high standards or want things a certain way, so we set ourselves up for letdowns, for failures. For a husband and wife to assess their personal sense of failure is to begin to bring a healing into their lives.

Courage to Share

Courage is needed in order to share. We are by nature, like nature . . . closed, until we bloom. Each of us has a protective skin. Making ourselves vulnerable is not easy. Only the end result of unity is worthwhile. Writing gives impetus to the courageous.

A certain couple was making a Marriage Encounter. After the time for writing was over, the husband and wife got together to exchange notebooks and share. In their first encounter, the husband had nothing written down. In their second encounter, they shared reasonably well, but again he had written nothing. In their third meeting, she finally asked him why he had not written, especially since he was enjoying the weekend and had much to share. He told her that early in their marriage he had asked her to take care of the checking account and all of their correspondence. And at work his secretary took care of the typing and letters. Then he told her that since childhood he had been a terrible speller, and that throughout adulthood he had arranged things so that his writing was at an absolute minimum. Just by sharing this with his wife he felt that a load was being lifted from him. She said that she could easily decipher anything he wrote and not to worry. What many couples write to each other during their engagement, this couple began to write years later.

Feeling Words

The following list of feelings is offered as a help for writing and expressing your feelings. In doing your writing, look over this list and use the words that really tell how you feel.

Affectionate	Calm	Defiant
Afraid	Carefree	Dependent
Aggressive	Cautious	Depressed
Airy	Choked up	Determined
Alarmed	Close	Dishonest
Angry	Cold	Distant
Anxious	Comforted	Dominant
Appealing	Compassionate	Dull
Ashamed	Confident	
	Confused	
Beaten	Contemptuous	Ecstatic
Belligerent	Contented	Edgy
Bewildered	Cooperative	Embarrassed
Bored	Courageous	Empathetic
Breathless		Enraged
Burdened	Dead-eyed	Envious
Bushed	Deferential	Estranged

Evasive
Excited

Fearful
Firm
Frisky
Frustrated

Giddy
Grateful
Grief-stricken
Grumpy
Guilty
Gutless

Happy
Hard
Hopeful
Hopeless
Horrified
Humble

Immobilized
Impatient
Inadequate
Independent
Insecure
Irritated
Itchy

Jealous
Joyful

Light
Locked in
Lonely
Loving

Mixed up

Nauseated

Open

Panicky
Paralyzed
Peaceful
Played out
Pleased
Powerless
Proud

Quiet

Relaxed
Resentful
Respectful

Sad
Scared
Seductive

Self-assured
Sexy
Silly
Soft
Spineless
Stretched
Strong
Submissive
Sunshiny
Surprised
Sweaty
Sympathetic

Talkative
Taut
Tender
Tense
Terrified
Thankful
Threatened
Thrilled
Timid
Tolerant
Torn
Two-faced

Uptight

Vacant

Warm
Weepy

How Do I Feel. . . ?

Note: Every day, answer one of the questions below. (Change the question to anything you want.) Separately, write your answer to the chosen question. Sit together with your spouse and read each other's letter. Finally, in your own words, tell each other what you wrote.

First day: How do I feel about writing down my feelings and sharing them with you?

Second day: How do I feel about going out with you in the evening?

Third day: How do I feel about going out alone in the evening?

Fourth day: How do I feel when you seem bored?

Fifth day: How do I feel about moving from where we are now living?

Sixth day: How do I feel about shopping for furniture?

Seventh day: How do I feel about sharing my failures?

Eighth day: How do I feel about sharing feelings from the past?

Ninth day: How do I feel when I am around strangers?

Tenth day: How do I feel about spending meaningful time with the children?

6
The Trusting Level

Harry and Ellen — Becoming Comfortable

Harry is well into his 20s and is not yet married. He dates on occasion but finds few girls who really interest him. He makes it to most of the office parties, but he is by nature quiet and rather shy. He becomes bored with the chatter of the parties and usually winds up in the corner all alone. By 11 o'clock he is usually home and in bed.

Ellen has reached her mid-20s. Most of her friends have married and are having children. She is very attractive and loves going to parties and having a good time. At any gathering an ample amount of men are usually around her. Ellen loves it. Protected at home by her parents, she lets her folks make most of her decisions — be it the dress that looks best on her or what to fix for supper.

Harry and Ellen work at the same office. He finds her

attractive to the point that he is afraid to approach her, let alone ask her out. She notices his quiet strength, and she goes out of her way every day to give Harry a special smile. One day they have lunch together in the cafeteria and Harry asks Ellen out to a party that weekend. She accepts. He has a marvelous time. All kinds of interesting people gather around them. Ellen looks great next to him. He hardly has to say a word. They dance and have a grand time until the wee hours of the morning.

Harry continues to invite Ellen out, asking her where she would like to go. She tells him to decide. The girls at work die with envy when they learn about the classy restaurants and shows Harry takes Ellen to. When they are out together Harry and Ellen easily draw others around them, and always seem to have a good time. Everyone says they make an excellent pair. They both feel very comfortable together.

Ellen and Harry become engaged and are married. But once they are married, several dark clouds begin to appear. Harry is content to sit at home. He enjoys relaxing. Ellen finds married life to her liking, but misses her social life. When they go out to a party, Harry is jealous because Ellen continues to draw men around her and does not seem to mind their presence. He accuses her of flirting. As a result of this, they end up staying home.

While they were dating, Harry enjoyed making all the decisions — where to go and what to do. Now that they are married, he has to determine their weekend plans, their budget, their daily routine, etc. By the end of their first year of marriage, Harry and Ellen are snapping at each other. Harry never wants to go anywhere with her. Ellen can't make her mind up about what side of the bed to get up on.

Comfortable Together

Most people get married because they feel comfortable together. In the case of Harry and Ellen, she drew attention to them at parties and thus made him feel important. He made decisions for her which she had let her parents make since she was born. Their relationship was comfortable. This proved to be the tip of the iceberg. Once married, Harry could not stand her continual popularity, especially at parties, or her inability to make even simple decisions. And Ellen could not stand staying home all the time.

Qualities admired in the other person before marriage can often prove annoying, if not destructive, once married. For example:

Promptness in dating can become nagging about being late.

Neatness in dating can become compulsive tidiness later.

Interest can become prying and being nosy or overbearing.

Talkativeness can become endless chatter and rambling.

Quiet strength can become stone coldness and dull withdrawals.

The strange fact of life is: We are all icebergs. We all have so much beneath our surface. In dating, only the tip of the iceberg is generally seen. In marriage the entire person becomes present.

Feeling uncomfortable, where once I felt comfortable, does not signal the end of the relationship. Rather it should signal the beginning of the marriage. Since I am no longer single, and hopefully not a married single, I have to discover, no matter how painful, what my flirting, my jealousy, my indecisiveness, my withdrawing, my promptness, my neatness, my prying, my talkativeness, or my coldness do to my partner. Often I do not realize the tremendous constructive or destructive resources I possess. For example:

"I flirt because I'm afraid to encounter people ... I'd rather be a butterfly."

"I am jealous because I'd like to control my partner's behavior."

"I am indecisive because I've never had the chance to prove myself."

"I withdraw because the world out there often tears me apart."

"I am prompt because I get nervous thinking I'll be late and people will look at me."

"I pry because I'm uneasy unless I know where I stand."

"I am talkative because then I don't have to get serious."

"I am cold because my outlook is so often negative and I hate to come on that way . . . so I stay quiet and cold."

Once Harry and Ellen can uncover these feelings in themselves and confidently share them through dialogue, then they can begin to grow again as friends and lovers in their marriage.

Trusting You

Trust is a faith, a belief in myself and in you. Even though I may flirt or get jealous, I am still O.K. . . . you are still O.K. I may not like the way you are acting, but at least we've had the courage to dialogue about it. Most of all I see how my actions or words trigger feelings in you. In marriage it is easy to outgrow the other person or to go in different directions. When I trust the rightness of our being together, then roses can bloom, even in the middle of the desert.

Trust begins to happen as the marriage starts to mature. At this point, we have both experienced how much we can love each other, or how much hurt we can inflict on each other. We have both felt the power we possess to be tender and gentle or to be angry and cruel. I can be either — gentle or cruel — as I so choose to be. I have to have a basic trust that my self-revelation to you won't come back to me in a hurting way or be used against me in an argument. Once I have shared that I am often indecisive or flirtatious or jealous, any of these can wash ashore during an explosive moment. There is no doubt about the risk involved in trusting you with myself. I could get hurt! This is true. It is also possible that I could be loved!

Seekers and Avoiders

What often hinders the trusting level in marriage is that one person is a "seeker" while the other is being an "avoider." So much of life at home unfolds this way:

"I want to talk." . . . "I want to be quiet and read the paper."

"I want to go out for a walk." . . . "I want to stay home and relax."

"I want to make love." . . . "I'm not feeling up to it tonight."

"I want to go out to eat." . . . "I would rather eat at home."

"I want to enroll the children for music lessons." . . . "I would rather save the money."

Polarities like these are almost certain to develop soon into the marriage. All of the common interests and the doing of things together before marriage cannot shield a couple from the fact that they are both very different. As these differences materialize, the roles of "seeker" and "avoider" will be played out. This has happened in each of the scenarios portrayed:

Jamie sought to put new life into their marriage through the intimate dinner; Stu unknowingly avoided calling her to say he would be late.

Betty wanted to go shopping; Alan was tired and wanted to watch TV.

Milt wanted to talk about the day they had had at his mother's; Olive was busy thinking about the next day.

Derek was up and doing things early on Saturday morning; Bretta was in the habit of sleeping late.

Fran wanted to go out in the evening to discussions; Earl had a long day and wanted to spend time with the children.

Ellen wanted to continue to go out to parties; Harry was jealous of her and was more interested in staying at home.

In all of these instances, none of the partners considered themselves the "avoider." They were all doing what they thought was best. No moral judgment need be passed on any of the above. But good feelings of trust are more apt to be experienced and shared when both partners become "seekers" (or "avoiders") in any given situation.

The *Us* Factor

One and one equal two. We learned this simple mathematical fact early in life. Yet this mathematical fact may not always be true. One and one in marriage may equal *more* than two. The *Us* Factor is based on the principle of synergism, that one and one do not necessarily equal two, but may equal three, or four, or more. The total effect of two people in marriage may be greater than the two of them taken individually. This happens in marriage when two people possess each other in love . . . when a permanent bridge has been erected over the dividing walls.

The *Us* Factor is a third entity that two lovers in marriage create. It is greater than themselves and it binds them together in a way that no legal document ever could. What comes into existence is a "me" in you and a "you" in me. What was once yours is now mine. We are entirely each other's.

Two threads taken separately cannot bear much weight or strain. Yet taken together and entwined, they are able to carry so much more than taken separately. So it is in marriage. As two lives become entwined, a couple is able to overcome the daily trials and experience the joys of marital love. The *Us* has now become the most exciting part of life together. The *Us* changes attitudes and behavior of both partners. The *Us* Factor fosters a continuing openness in the relationship. There is now a commonality of being from which new life flows. "United we stand" gives a new thrust to life.

Each of us has stood on railroad tracks aware of how separate the two tracks were. Although important loads are carried on them each day, they remain separate. But on the horizon the two tracks seem to meet. The *Us* Factor brings the two tracks of two lives together, not on some distant horizon, but in the here-and-now where life can be shared and enjoyed.

How Do I Feel. . . ?

Note: Every day, answer one of the questions below. (Change the question to anything you want.) Separately, write your answer to the chosen question. Sit together with your spouse and read each other's letter. Finally, in your own words, tell each other what you wrote.

First day:	How do I feel when I am comfortable?
Second day:	How do I feel when I am jealous?
Third day:	How do I feel about being neat or tidy?
Fourth day:	How do I feel when I am accepted and cared for?
Fifth day:	How do I feel when I am put down?
Sixth day:	How do I feel when I am the "seeker" or the "avoider"?
Seventh day:	How do I feel about our strength as a couple?
Eighth day:	How do I feel when we are apart?
Ninth day:	How do I feel about trusting you?
Tenth day:	How do I feel about our being different?

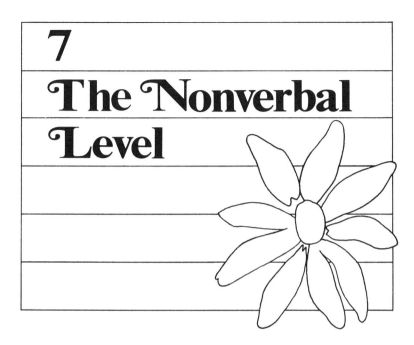

7
The Nonverbal Level

Sally and Roland — A New Marriage

Roland stood off in the corner by himself. He wanted to be alone, even if only for a moment or two. Just hours before, he had buried his son. Roland's memory drifted back three years to that day in the doctor's office. The doctor had sat the two of them down in his office and gave them the results of the tests: their son had leukemia; he had one to three years to live. The doctor had also remarked that they should take special care of their marriage: in his experience, many of the parents of children with leukemia separated once the child died.

That was three years ago. Roland had hardly heard the words the doctor said about their marriage. But those three years had taken their toll ... always rushing to the hospital ... hope after hope dashed ... hurried meals ... the house always a mess . . . their other children often staying with neighbors. . . .

As he looked across the room, Roland spied Sally. He felt that he loved her tremendously, more than ever before. But he realized that he really didn't know her any more.

From across the room, Sally caught her husband backing off by himself. She felt such compassion for him. How he had suffered. How drained he had become. His business hopes had long been put aside. Not once until the day of death had Sally seen Roland cry. She knew that he cried. The half-smile he flashed her as he walked into the hospital room after work often tried to hide his two very red eyes. She too cried, but never in front of Roland. They both felt they had to be strong for each other. Now the time for that had ended.

Sally, too, remembered what the doctor had said three years before. A new daily grind would be beginning. She prayed that she would not take out her hurts and her grief on her husband. Once again Sally prayed for strength.

Are We a Pair?

Moments like the one described above are what make a marriage. Little or nothing can be said. Yet at the same time the partners can feel tremendous love, a great aloneness, or both. The nonverbal level becomes the moment of truth. In the song "Send in the Clowns," Judy Collins asks: "Are we a pair?" Sally and Roland also ask, "Are we a pair?" All masks are stripped away. They see themselves and each other as they are.

Such moments occur infrequently, yet often enough in marriage. The moment may be a pregnancy, the birth of a baby, the loss of a parent or loved one, the loss of a job, a miscarriage, a transfer or a move. Whatever the occasion, the moment reveals whether we are truly a pair or merely married singles.

"It was at my father's funeral. I reached out to grab my wife's hand. Her hand tensed. She pulled back. She gave me her handkerchief and asked me to stop crying."

"I put my hand on her stomach filled with our child and I feel such love. We have so much going for us. Every time she moves in bed my heart moves with the love I feel. Why should I be so fortunate as to have such an understanding and caring woman?"

A look, a glance, a touch, a kiss, a squeeze, an embrace, or a withdrawal — these are the telltale signs whether this is truly a marriage or not. If it is, then this final level of nonverbal communication is a celebration of a penetrating marriage. If it is not, then a full rending is likely to occur. This does not mean that a separation or a divorce is in the offing. It does mean that a spiritual divorce has occurred even if the spouses continue to live together.

The Possible Dream

What can be done? Since these are truly "critical" moments in life and in marriage, often enough seemingly impossible things can begin to happen. Many times I have seen a spouse get serious about counseling or working to better a marriage only when the divorce papers are served. A divorce is no longer seen as an idle threat. The past is coming to an end. Reality strikes. When this reality finally hits home, the nonverbal level often gives way to the verbal:

"We've finally cleared the air. What we've both been feeling for years, but not saying, is finally coming out. I hope it's not too late."

At this nonverbal level partners can plunge beneath the surface and sexual levels of their daily existence to a true sharing. For example:

Sally:

"How I ached to see our home being torn apart by our boy's illness and death. I felt helpless . . . I had nothing to give to anyone. I was numb, merely surviving. More than anything, I wanted to give myself to you. But after giving night and day to our son, I had nothing left."

Roland:

"I was so beset by fear. I've been a nervous wreck. Every time I saw you these past three years, I've wanted to hold you, to squeeze you with all of my might. But I was afraid. For some reason I was afraid that you too would leave me like our son was doing. I lost so much faith in living. Will you help me to start believing again?"

Bringing the nonverbal level to the verbal level with tenderness and love promotes a great healing. In the words of Christ, the Great Healer: "The girl is not dead. She is only sleeping" (Mark 5:39). The same is true of wondrous feelings after years of marriage. "Your feelings are not dead. They are only sleeping, waiting to be awakened." Deep words of faith and love have this healing power.

Why and How?

All of the other levels of marriage are preliminary to this last stage. For when there is no sound or noise, I am confronted with reflecting and asking myself:

"Why do I want to go on living?"

"How do I want to go on living?"

Cicero once said that the only real questions are the ultimate questions. This holds true for marriage. The success or failure of my marriage cannot be measured against anybody or anything else — my job, the children, or someone else's marriage. In responding to these two questions, the merely surface and sexual levels of marriage give way to all that has been hiding beneath them. There can be an eruption, almost like a volcano — an eruption of love.

For when I adequately determine why I want to go on living, the clouds seem to disappear and questions begin to have answers. Many others have set a purpose for my life, but now I have found a purpose all my own. No longer is my life going in every direction. Now it is taking one straight and true course:

"I, Roland, take you, Sally, to be my wife. I promise to be true to you in good times and in bad, in sickness and in health. I will love you and honor you all the days of my life."

"I, Sally, take you, Roland, to be my husband. I promise to be true to you in good times and in bad, in sickness and in health. I will love you and honor you all the days of my life."

Untangling the Thread

Life often seems like a tangled ball of thread. In answering the question "*Why* do I want to go on living?" life begins to become untangled and the threads of two lives become intertwined.

"*How* do I want to go on living?" must be seen in light of a common, shared vision. I choose not to live life alone. I want to share my life, even my tears, if necessary. Just because the past was too often separate, this does not mean that the future has to be the same. Two separate vantage points can become one vision. The nonverbal level can become verbal:

"Many of the things I wanted to say or do I formerly never had the time for or the courage to do. If you will help me, I now have the time and I will find the courage."

"Every day for years I got up and poured myself out for the job and the kids. Lately I've felt lifeless after years of this. Help me to find new life and new meaning to my existence."

When do we really begin to live our lives? When does a marriage begin? At the altar?. . . or years later? The Christ who rose from the tomb on Easter morning was gloriously scarred by all the world had done to him. Marriage too leaves many scars. These scars can be healed and actually become beautiful when a spouse recognizes them, and loves the person who wears them, and believes in the mutual love that can daily be shared.

The Tree of Life

In the Garden of Eden, alongside the first man and woman, there was planted a tree. That tree can be compared to marriage — the tree of everyday life. As with Adam and Eve, we too go after the fruit of that tree. We want to see the *Surface* blooming, to taste the *Physical* enjoyment. But the all-important trunk sustains its branches, leaves, and fruit. For that trunk has rings of *Friendship, Sharing,* and *Trusting* that go from top to bottom. And its many roots of faith and love will, in a *Nonverbal* way, cause it to reach fruition in due season.

For it is marriage in all of its dimensions that is for us, as it was for Adam and Eve, the very tree of life itself. It is for us to plumb marriage to its depths and discover the wondrous meaning of God's creative plan.

How Do I Feel. . . ?

Note: Every day, answer one of the questions below. (Change the question to anything you want.) Separately, write your answer to the chosen question. Sit together with your spouse and read each other's letter. Finally, in your own words, tell each other what you wrote.

First day: How do I feel about crying?

Second day: How do I feel when we have to face a crisis?

Third day: How do I feel about our nonverbal communication?

Fourth day: How do I feel when I admit to my fears?

Fifth day: How do I feel when you heal me?

Sixth day: How do I feel about "Why I want to go on living"?

Seventh day: How do I feel about "How I want to go on living"?

Eighth day: How do I feel when you help me?

Ninth day: How do I feel when we are apart?

Tenth day: How do I feel when we have time together?

Other helpful publications from Liguori:

PRAYERS FOR MARRIED COUPLES
by Renee Bartkowski
$3.95

UNDER ONE ROOF
Good News for Families
by Vernie Dale
$1.50

FAMILY PLANNING
A Guide for Exploring the Issues
by Charles and Elizabeth Balsam
$4.95

THE NINE-MONTH MIRACLE
A Journal for the Mother-to-Be
by Carrie J. Heiman
$4.95

SEX AND MARRIAGE
A Catholic Perspective
by John M. Hamrogue, C.SS.R.
$2.95

HOW TO IMPROVE YOUR RELATIONSHIPS
by Ralph F. Ranieri
$2.50

HOW TO SURVIVE BEING MARRIED TO A CATHOLIC
A Frank and Honest Guide to Catholic Attitudes,
Beliefs, and Practices
A Redemptorist Pastoral Publication
$3.95

Order from your local bookstore or write to:
Liguori Publications
Box 060, Liguori, MO 63057-9999
(Please add $1.00 for postage and handling for
orders under $5.00; $1.50 for orders over $5.00.)